T'shai's Hair Journey

Books & Things Publishing, LLC
4410 Brookfield Corporate Dr. #220149
Chantilly, VA 20153

DEDICATION

To my deceased father, Ervin Rouse, and to my grandparents and T'shai's great grandparents, Elizabeth and Edwin Rouse. And to all of our extended family that helped raise me in Salazar Trace, Point Fortin, Trinidad.

Once upon a time, there was a little girl named T'shai. She was born in Brooklyn, her mom migrated from Trinidad and her father is from Jamaica.

T'shai loved her life in Brooklyn, but she hated one thing about herself: her hair.

T'shai's hair was thick as wool and unmanageable, and she absolutely hated it.

She would always complain about how difficult it was to comb and style her hair. She always wished she had straight, smooth hair like her friends at school.

Her mom T'shura had long locs, and she loved her hair, but T'shai didn't understand why and how.

One day, T'shura decided to make a change. She created a brand for hair products called Butterflies Natural.

T'shura gained all her knowledge about natural hair products from her deceased grandmother, Elizabeth.

So she created a store that sold all-natural hair products for people with all kinds of hair.

T'shai would often go to the store after school and help her mom with the customers.

One day,
T'shura noticed
how sad and upset
T'shai was about
her hair.

She took T'shai aside and said, "Your hair is beautiful, my girl. You just need to learn how to take care of it."

Then she showed T'shai all the different products in the store that could help her manage her hair.

T'shai was hesitant to try the new products at first, but her mom convinced her to give it a chance.

She used the shampoo, conditioner, and leave-in conditioner that her mom recommended. After the first wash, T'shai could already see a difference.

Her hair was easier to comb, and it looked shinier and healthier than before.

As she continued to use the Butterflies Natural Products, T'shai started to love her hair more and more.

She realized that her hair was unique and beautiful, just like her mom's locs. T'shai even started to experiment with different hairstyles and hair accessories.

Before she knew it, T'shai's hair became her pride and joy. She loved showing it off to her friends and family,

and she even helped her mom at the store by demonstrating how to use the products on different hair types.

T'shura was proud of Tshai and looked lovingly into her eyes and said, "T'shai, always remember that you are beautiful just the way you are. Your hair is unique and special, just like you. Embrace your curls, for they are a part of what makes you shine.

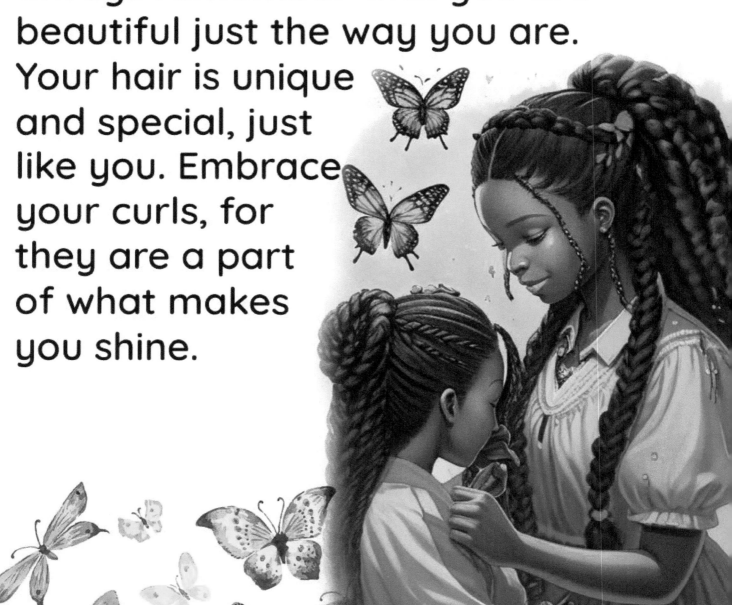

...You are strong, you are loved, and you are absolutely amazing. Don't ever let anyone make you doubt your worth. Believe in yourself, my dear, because you are capable of achieving anything you set your mind to."

And so, T'shai's hair journey ended happily ever after. She learned to love herself just the way she is.

As she learned that there was a whole world of natural hair products out there waiting for her to discover.

Thanks to Butterflies Natural, T'shai was able to embrace her natural beauty and feel confident the way she is.

But as T'shai embraced her natural hair and learned to love herself, she realized that her story was not just her own. It was a story that resonated with girls from all different cultures and backgrounds.

T'shai wanted to spread a message of self-acceptance and love to all those girls out there who may have felt the same insecurities she once did. She knew that true beauty came from within, and that embracing one's uniqueness was the key to happiness.

From that day forward, T'shai made it her mission to inspire and empower all girls to accept themselves and love themselves just the way they were.

Because when we celebrate our differences, we create a world that is colorful, diverse, and truly beautiful.

THE END

Printed in the USA
CPSIA information can be obtained
at www.ICGtesting.com
LVHW060317220224
772478LV00005B/12